SPINK'S

GUIDE TO THE WEARING
OF
ORDERS, DECORATIONS AND MEDALS

——————— • ———————

Stephen Connelly

SPINK & SON LTD.
LONDON
1986

ISBN 0907605 20 6

By appointment
to Her Majesty The Queen
Medallists
SPINK & SON LTD. LONDON

By appointment
to H.R.H. The Duke of Edinburgh
Medallists
SPINK & SON LTD. LONDON

By appointment
to H.R.H. The Prince of Wales
Medallists
SPINK & SON LTD. LONDON

Spink ~ 0207-563 ~ 4000

Spink & Son Ltd. King Street, St James's, London SW1Y 6QS.

Tel: 01-930 7888 (24hrs) Telex: 916711 [Coins + medals] Coy

Spink & Son (Australia) Pty Ltd
53 Martin Place
Sydney, NSW 2000, Australia
Telephone: Sydney 27 5571
Telex: Australia 27283

Spink Modern Collections Ltd
PO Box 222, 29-35 Gladstone Road
Croydon, Surrey CR9 3RP
Telephone: 01-689 5131
Telex: 949750

Spink & Son Ltd
(Medal Manufacturing Division)
587 Kingston Road
Raynes Park, London SW20

Spink & Son (Australia) Pty Ltd
MLC Building, 303 Collins Street
Melbourne, Victoria 3000,
Australia
Telephone: 61-2799
Telex: Australia 134825

Spink & Son, Numismatics Ltd
Löwenstrasse 65
8001 Zürich, Switzerland
Telephone: Zürich 01-221 1885
Telex: 8121009 SPK CH

THE SPINK
NUMISMATIC CIRCULAR

Published monthly, except January and August.
A special *Medal Supplement* is available for medal
collectors only in January.

A listing, with illustrations, of coins, medals, banknotes
and associated books for the discerning collector.

Annual subscription for the United Kingdom and Europe
is £8. The rest of the world (by air only) £20, or $US
equilvalent. Subscriptions may be paid to the overseas
offices of Spink & Son Ltd in Australia and Switzerland.

The Medal Division of Spink & Son Ltd offers the undermentioned services:-

(1) Design and manufacture of Orders, Decorations and Medals for the British Commonwealth and Foreign Governments.

(2) Manufacture of an extensive range of miniature medals for most countries of the world.

(3) Mounting for wear and renovating full size and miniature awards.

(4) Stockists of a large selection of awards both for collectors and as replacements for those awards that have been lost.

(5) Glass-fronted display cases for private and museum purposes.

(6) Stockists and publishers of leading reference books.

(7) Purchasers of surplus Orders, Decorations and Medals of the world to satisfy the growing number of students and collectors.

I gratefully acknowledge the help given to me by the undermentioned
authorities:—

Major-General D. H. G. Rice, C.V.O., C.B.E.
Secretary
The Central Chancery of the Orders of Knighthood
St James's Palace
LONDON
SW1A 1BG

S. W. F. Martin Esq., L.V.O./A. G. L. Turner Esq., L.V.O.
H.M. Diplomatic Service
Protocol Department
Foreign and Commonwealth Office
King Charles Street
LONDON   SW1A 2AH

NAVY   Lieutenant Commander J. A. Holt, R.N.
The Flag Lieutenant to the Admiralty Board
Ministry of Defence
Main Building
Whitehall
LONDON
SW1A 2HB

ARMY   Colonel L. L. Fleming, M.B.E., M.C.
Ministry of Defence
PS 12B
Empress State Building
Lillie Road
Fulham
LONDON   SW6 1TR

RAF   Squadron Leader G. J. S. Gardner, R.A.F. Rtd.
Ministry of Defence
P1b (Cer) (RAF), Room 331
Adastral House
Theobalds Road
LONDON
WC1X 8RU

I would also like to express my appreciation of the advice freely given by
Edward Joslin, who has never hesitated to make suggestions to improve the
contents of this guide, the first of its kind.

S. J. Connelly

Foreword

The policy of acknowledging the services of citizens by awarding them Orders, Decorations and Medals has developed over the last 200 years or so, and today, very many people, in all walks of life are proud recipients of one or more medals. However, there has been no publication generally available to inform them as to when or how the various awards are to be worn.

Spink & Son Limited, who can justly claim to have the world's most comprehensive Medal Department, has now made an attempt to overcome the lack of knowledge in this area.

The author, Stephen Connelly, who has specialised in this particular field for some ten years by virtue of the fact that he has been in charge of our reception area, meets a large number of recipients of such awards. In this capacity he has gained a knowledge which is second to none.

Edward Joslin
Director, Spink & Son Ltd

Table of Contents

THE ORDER OF PRECEDENCE

The following list shows the order in which Orders, Decorations and Medals should be worn in the United Kingdom, certain countries of the Commonwealth, and in the overseas territories, as issued by The Central Chancery of the Orders of Knighthood on 28th October 1983.

Victoria Cross
George Cross
Most Noble Order of the Garter
Most Ancient and Most Noble Order of the Thistle
Most Illustrious Order of St. Patrick
Knights Grand Cross, The Most Honourable Order of the Bath (G.C.B.)
Order of Merit
Baronet's Badge
Knight Grand Commander, The Most Exalted Order of the Star of India
    (G.C.S.I.)
Knights Grand Cross, The Most Distinguished Order of St. Michael and St.
    George (G.C.M.G.)
Knight Grand Commander, The Most Eminent Order of the
    Indian Empire (G.C.I.E.)
The Order of the Crown of India
Knights Grand Cross, The Royal Victorian Order (G.C.V.O.)
Knights Grand Cross, The Most Excellent Order of the British Empire (G.B.E.)
Order of the Companions of Honour (C.H.)
Knight Commander, The Most Honourable Order of the Bath (K.C.B.)
Knight Commander, The Most Exalted Order of the Star of India (K.C.S.I.)
Knight Commander, The Most Distinguished Order of St. Michael and St.
    George (K.C.M.G.)
Knight Commander, The Most Eminent Order of the Indian Empire (K.C.I.E.)
Knight Commander, The Royal Victorian Order (K.C.V.O.)
Knight Commander, The Most Excellent Order of the British Empire (K.B.E.)
Knight Bachelor's Badge
Companion, The Most Honourable Order of the Bath (C.B.)
Companion, The Most Exalted Order of the Star of India (C.S.I.)
Companion, The Most Distinguished Order of St. Michael and St. George (C.M.G.)
Companion, The Most Eminent Order of the Indian Empire (C.I.E.)
Commander, The Royal Victorian Order (C.V.O.)
Commander, The Most Excellent Order of the British Empire (C.B.E.)
Distinguished Service Order (D.S.O.)
Lieutenant, The Royal Victorian Order (L.V.O.)
Officer, The Most Excellent Order of the British Empire (O.B.E.)
Imperial Service Order (I.S.O.)
Member, The Royal Victorian Order (M.V.O.)
Member, The Most Excellent Order of the British Empire (M.B.E.)
Indian Order of Merit—Military

Decorations

Royal Red Cross, Class 1
Distinguished Service Cross
Military Cross
Distinguished Flying Cross

Air Force Cross
Royal Red Cross, Class II
Order of British India
Kaisar-I-Hind Medal
Order of St. John

Gallantry and Distinguished Conduct Medals

Union of South Africa Queen's Medal for Bravery in gold
Distinguished Conduct Medal
Conspicuous Gallantry Medal
Conspicuous Gallantry Medal (Flying)
George Medal
Queen's Police Medal for Gallantry
Queen's Fire Service Medal for Gallantry
Royal West African Frontier Force Distinguished Conduct Medal
King's African Rifles Distinguished Conduct Medal
Indian Distinguished Service Medal
Union of South Africa Queen's Medal for Bravery in silver
Distinguished Service Medal
Military Medal
Distinguished Flying Medal
Air Force Medal
Royal Ulster Constabulary Medal
Medal for Saving Life at Sea
Indian Order of Merit (Civil)
Indian Police Medal for Gallantry
Ceylon Police Medal for Gallantry
Sierra Leone Police Medal for Gallantry
Sierra Leone Fire Brigades Medal for Gallantry
Colonial Police Medal for Gallantry
Queen's Gallantry Medal
Royal Victorian Medal (gold, silver and bronze)
British Empire Medal
Canada Medal
Queen's Police Medal for Distinguished Service
Queen's Fire Service Medal for Distinguished Service
Queen's Medal for Chiefs
War Medals, including the UN Medals—in order of date of campaign for which
    awarded
Polar Medals—in order of date of award
Imperial Service Medal

Police Medals for Valuable Services

Indian Police Medal for Meritorious Service
Ceylon Police Medal for Merit
Sierra Leone Police Medal for Meritorious Service
Sierra Leone Fire Brigades Medal for Meritorious Service
Colonial Police Medal for Meritorious Service
Badge of Honour

Jubilee, Coronation and Durbar Medals

Queen Victoria's Jubilee Medal 1887 (gold, silver and bronze)
Queen Victoria's Police Jubilee Medal 1887
Queen Victoria's Jubilee Medal 1897 (gold, silver and bronze)
Queen Victoria's Police Jubilee Medal 1897
Queen Victoria's Commemoration Medal 1900 (Ireland)
King Edward VII's Coronation 1902
King Edward VII's Police Coronation 1902
King Edward VII's Durbar 1903 (gold, silver and bronze)
King Edward VII's Police Medal 1903 (Scotland)
King's Visit Commemoration Medal 1903 (Ireland)
King George V's Coronation Medal 1911
King George V's Police Coronation Medal 1911
King George V's Visit Police Commemoration Medal 1911 (Ireland)
King George V's Durbar Medal 1911 (gold, silver and bronze)
King George V's Silver Jubilee Medal 1935
King George VI's Coronation Medal 1937
Queen Elizabeth II's Coronation Medal 1953
Queen Elizabeth II's Silver Jubilee Medal 1977
King George V's Long and Faithful Service Medal
King George VI's Long and Faithful Service Medal
Queen Elizabeth II's Long and Faithful Service Medal

Efficiency and Long Service Decorations and Medals

Medal for Meritorious Service
The Medal for Long Service and Good Conduct, Army
Naval Long Service and Good Conduct Medal
Medal for Meritorious Service (Royal Navy 1918-28)
Indian Long Service and Good Conduct Medal (for Europeans of Indian Army)
Indian Meritorious Service Medal (for Europeans of Indian Army)
Royal Marines Meritorious Service Medal (1849-1947)
Royal Air Force Meritorious Service Medal 1918-28
Royal Air Force Long Service and Good Conduct Medal
Ulster Defence Regiment Long Service and Good Conduct Medal
Indian Long Service and Good Conduct Medal (Indian Army)
Royal West African Frontier Force Long Service and Good Conduct Medal
Royal Sierra Leone Military Forces Long Service and Good Conduct Medal
King's African Rifles Long Service and Good Conduct Medal
Indian Meritorious Service Medal (for Indian Army)
Police Long Service and Good Conduct Medal
Fire Brigade Long Service and Good Conduct Medal
African Police Medal for Meritorious Service
Royal Canadian Mounted Police Long Service Medal
Ceylon Police Long Service Medal
Ceylon Fire Services Long Service Medal
Sierra Leone Police Long Service Medal
Colonial Police Long Service Medal
Sierra Leone Fire Brigade Long Service Medal
Mauritius Police Long Service and Good Conduct Medal

Mauritius Fire Service Long Service and Good Conduct Medal
Mauritius Prisons Service Long Service and Good Conduct Medal
Colonial Fire Brigades Long Service Medal
Colonial Prison Service Medal
Army Emergency Reserve Decoration
Volunteer Officers' Decoration
Volunteer Long Service Medal
Volunteer Officers' Decoration (for India and the Colonies)
Volunteer Long Service Medal (for India and the Colonies)
Colonial Auxiliary Forces Officers' Decoration
Colonial Auxiliary Forces Long Service Medal
Medal for Good Shooting (Naval)
Militia Long Service Medal
Imperial Yeomanry Long Service Medal
Territorial Decoration
Ceylon Armed Services Long Service Medal
Efficiency Decoration
Territorial Efficiency Medal
Efficiency Medal
Special Reserve Long Service and Good Conduct Medal
Decoration for Officers of the Royal Naval Reserve
Decoration for Officers of the Royal Naval Volunteer Reserve
Royal Naval Reserve Long Service and Good Conduct Medal
Royal Naval Volunteer Reserve Long Service and Good Conduct Medal
Royal Naval Auxiliary Sick Berth Reserve Long Service and Good Conduct
    Medal
Royal Fleet Reserve Long Service and Good Conduct Medal
Royal Naval Wireless Auxiliary Reserve Long Service and Good Conduct Medal
Royal Naval Auxiliary Service Medal
Air Efficiency Award
Ulster Defence Regiment Medal
Queen's Medal (for Champion Shots of the Royal Navy and Royal Marines)
Queen's Medal (for Champion Shots of the New Zealand Naval Forces)
Queen's Medal (for Champion Shots in the Military Forces)
Queen's Medal (for Champion Shots of the Air Forces)
Cadet Forces Medal
Coast Guard Auxiliary Service Long Service Medal
Special Constabulary Long Service Medal
Canadian Forces Decoration
Royal Observer Corps Medal
Civil Defence Long Service Medal
Rhodesia Medal
Royal Ulster Constabulary Service Medal
Union of South Africa Commemoration Medal
Indian Independence Medal
Pakistan Medal
Ceylon Armed Services Inauguration Medal
Ceylon Police Independence Medal (1948)
Sierra Leone Independence Medal

Jamaica Independence Medal
Uganda Independence Medal
Malawi Independence Medal
Fiji Independence Medal
Papua New Guinea Independence Medal
Solomon Islands Independence Medal
Service Medal of the Order of St. John
Badge of the Order of the League of Mercy
Voluntary Medical Service Medal
Women's Voluntary Service Medal
South African Medal for War Services
Colonial Special Constabulary Medal
Honorary Membership of Commonwealth Orders (instituted by the Sovereign, in
    order of date of award)
Other Commonwealth Members, Orders, Decorations and Medals (instituted
    since 1949 otherwise than by the Sovereign, and awards by States of
    Malaysia and Brunei in order of date of award)
Foreign Orders in order of date of award
Foreign Decorations in order of date of award
Foreign Medals in order of date of award

The order in which Campaign Stars and Medals awarded for service during World War I and II are worn

1914 Star with dated 'Mons' clasp '15th AUGUST-22nd NOVEMBER 1914'
1914 Star
1914/15 Star
British War Medal
Mercantile Marine Medal
Victory Medal
Territorial Force War Medal

1939/45 Star
Atlantic Star
Air Crew Europe Star
Africa Star
Pacific Star
Burma Star
Italy Star
France and Germany Star
Defence Medal
Canadian Volunteer Service Medal
1939/45 War Medal
1939/45 Africa Service Medal of the Union of South Africa
India Service Medal
New Zealand War Service Medal
Southern Rhodesia Service Medal
Australian Service Medal

OCCASIONS WHEN
ORDERS, DECORATIONS AND MEDALS
ARE WORN

1) State occasions

2) Evening dress

1. State Occasions

1) On State occasions. This is:-
   (a) when the Sovereign or the Sovereign's representative is in attendance,
   (b) when a parade is held in honour of the Sovereign's birthday,
   (c) when specially ordered for a parade, ceremony, or entertainment at which a member of the Royal Family will be present.
   Guards on Royal Residencies,
   Royal Escorts,
   Guards of Honour,
   Ceremonial and Sovereign's Parades,
   Guards in London, Edinburgh, Balmoral, and on garrison duty as may be ordered by District Commanders,
   Military Funerals,
   Memorial Services,
   Parades which include a religious service,
   Courts Martial,
   When especially requested to do so.

2. Evening Dress

2) Occasions when insignia of Orders and miniature medals are worn with all types of evening dress:-
   (a) At all parties and dinners when any of the following members of the Royal Family are present:-
   Their Majesties The Queen and Queen Elizabeth, The Queen Mother.
   Their Royal Highnesses—1) The Duke of Edinburgh,
   2) The Prince and Princess of Wales,
   3) The Duke and Duchess of York,
   4) The Prince Edward,
   5) The Princess Anne, Mrs Mark Phillips,
   6) The Princess Margaret, Countess of Snowdon,
   7) Princess Alice, Duchess of Gloucester,
   8) The Duke and Duchess of Gloucester,
   9) The Duke and Duchess of Kent,
   10) Prince and Princess Michael of Kent,
   11) Princess Alexandra, The Honourable Mrs Angus Ogilvy.

(The host should notify all his guests if any of these members of the Royal Family will be present).

   (b) At all parties and dinners given in honour of Ambassadors and Ministers accredited to the Court of St. James's or unless otherwise notified by the Ambassador or Minister concerned.
   (c) At all official dinners and receptions including Royal Naval, Military and Air Force dinners, dinners of City Livery Companies and public dinners.

(d) On official occasions when hosted by:-
   HM Lord Lieutenant of a County, when within his county,
   The High Sheriff of a county, when within his county,
   Cabinet Ministers,
   Ex Cabinet Ministers,
   Knights of The Garter and Thistle,
   Great Officers of State and The Queen's Household,
   Lord Mayors and Mayor,
   Lord Provosts and Provosts.

On all the above occasions the invitation to a function should state 'Decorations' to indicate that the entertainment is an official one.

10

THE WEARING OF
ORDERS, DECORATIONS AND MEDALS
BY GENTLEMEN
WITH DIFFERENT STYLES OF
CIVILIAN DRESS

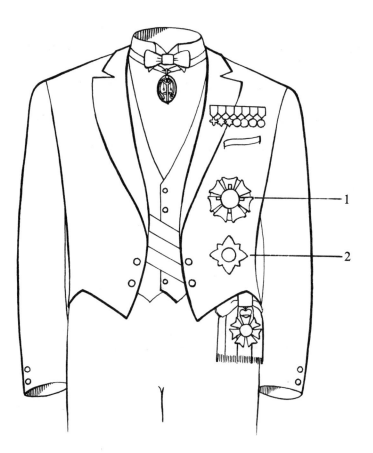

1

2

Evening Dress

1. Evening Dress

On all occasions when it is desired that Orders, Decorations and Medals are to be worn, invitations must state the following:-

"Evening Dress—Decorations"

Knights of The Order of The Garter, Thistle, and Knights Grand Cross, Knights Grand Commanders, Bailiffs Grand Cross

A half broad (sash) riband is worn under the black coat and over the white waistcoat (see pages 12 & 19). The Order badge rests on the appropriate hip, being attached beneath the bow.

On some occasions, such as a banquet held at the embassy of a foreign country, it would be more correct to wear the riband and badge of a lesser British or Foreign Order in which case these insignia should then take precedence. For example, someone attending a function given by the French Government would wear the Légion d'Honneur in pride of place over any British Orders, Decorations and Medals.

Only one broad (sash) riband is worn at any one time.

A maximum of four stars (of various classes) can be worn on the left hand side of the coat. The diagrams below show the positioning:-

Two Stars	*Three Stars*	*Four Stars*
1	1	1
2	2 3	2 3
		4

If the recipient is the holder of more than one award then miniature badges of all Orders, Decorations and Medals are worn from a medal bar on the left lapel (see page 52).

Collars are never worn.

Knights Commanders and Knights of Justice

A maximum of four stars (of various classes) may be worn in the same manner as previously described on the left side of the coat. One full size neck decoration is worn on a miniature width riband under the shirt collar, being suspended just below the position of the knot of the tie (see page 12). Miniature badges of all Orders, Decorations and Medals are worn from a medal bar on the left lapel (see page 52).

Companions and Commanders

One full size neck decoration is worn on a miniature width riband under the shirt collar, being suspended just below the knot of the tie (see page 12). Miniature badges of all Orders, Decorations and Medals are worn from a medal bar on the left lapel (see page 52).

Lieutenants, Officers, Members, Serving Brothers

Miniature badges of all Orders, Decorations and Medals are worn from a medal bar on the left lapel (see page 52)

Order of Merit, Companion of Honour, Baronet's Badge

These are all neck decorations which are worn on a miniature width riband under the shirt collar, being suspended just below the knot of the tie. The above mentioned Orders are never worn in miniature form.

Knight Bachelor's—See relevant chapter page 65.

Royal Victorian Chain

This chain and its badge may be worn around the neck in place of any neck badge. It is never worn in miniature form.

Dinner Jacket

2. Dinner Jacket

When it is desired that a dinner jacket and decorations are to be worn then invitations should state:-

"Dinner Jacket—Decorations"

The manner of wearing Orders, Decorations and Medals with a dinner jacket is as follows:-

Knights of The Order of The Garter and Thistle, Knights Grand Cross, Knights Grand Commanders, Bailiffs Grand Cross

Neither a collar nor broad (sash) riband is worn. One star is worn on the left breast. Miniature badges of all Orders, Decorations and Medals are worn from a medal bar on the left lapel (see page 52).

Knights Commanders, Knights of Justice

One star is worn on the left side of the coat. One full size neck decoration is worn on a miniature width riband, being worn under the shirt collar and suspended just below the position of the knot of the tie. Miniature badges of all Orders, Decorations and Medals are worn from a medal bar on the left lapel (see page 52).

Companions and Commanders

One full size neck decoration is worn on a miniature width riband, being worn under the shirt collar and suspended just below the position of the knot of the tie (see page 14). Miniature badges of all Orders, Decorations and Medals are worn from a medal bar on the left lapel (see page 52).

Lieutenants, Officers, Members, Serving Brothers

Miniature badges of all Orders, Decorations and Medals are worn from a medal bar on the left lapel (see page 52).

Order of Merit, Companion of Honour, Baronet's Badge

These are all neck decorations which are worn from a miniature width riband, being worn under the shirt collar and suspended just below the knot of the tie. The above mentioned Orders are never worn in miniature form.

Knight Bachelor's—see page 65.

The Royal Victorian Chain

This chain and its badge may be worn round the neck in place of any other neck decoration. It is never worn in miniature form.

3. Morning Dress

The occasions when Orders, Decorations and Medals are worn with morning dress are comparatively rare. If it is desired that they should be worn then guests are to be informed by the function organiser.

Knights of The Garter and Thistle, Knights Grand Cross, Knights Grand Commanders, Bailiffs Grand Cross

Collars are only worn if ordered for a special occasion. They are held in position by black thread or gold safety pins.

Broad (sash) ribands are not worn.

Normally, only one breast star is worn on the left hand side of the coat, but in exceptional circumstances, up to four may be worn in the manner previously discussed on page 13.

Knights Commanders, Knights of Justice

Normally, only one breast star is worn on the left hand side of the coat, but in exceptional circumstances, up to four may be worn in the manner previously discussed on page 13.

The associated neck decoration is not worn.

Companions, Commanders, Order of Merit, Companion of Honour, Baronet's Badge

One full size neck decoration may be worn on a miniature width riband, being worn under the shirt collar and suspended ¾in. below the knot, in front of the tie.

Lieutenants, Officers, Members

The full size decoration is worn, whether mounted singly or in a group, on the left side of the coat, with any additional full size medals and decorations.

The Royal Victorian Chain

This chain and it's badge may be worn around the neck in place of any other neck decoration.

4. Lounge Suits

It is not customary to wear collars, broad (sash) ribands, breast stars or the Royal Victorian Chain. One full size neck decoration is worn on a miniature width riband, being worn under the collar. It should hang ¾in. below the knot, in front of the tie.

Full size Orders, Decorations and Medals normally mounted on a medal bar should be worn on the left side during daytime functions, whilst miniature Orders, Decorations and Medals should be worn at events taking place in the evening, along with any neck decoration that the wearer is entitled to.

Lounge Suit

5. Overcoats

Usually, only full size Orders, Decorations and Medals which are mounted on a brooch are worn on the left side. Neck decorations are rarely worn except at the discretion of the holder on appropriate occasions such as Remembrance Day. They are worn in the same manner as described in section 4. Breast stars are never worn.

6. Collars

Collars of the Orders of Knighthood are worn by Knights of The Most Noble Order of The Garter and Knights of The Most Ancient and Most Noble Order of The Thistle, Knights Grand Cross, and at appropriate ceremonies when due notification has been given. They are never worn after sunset.

Only one collar is permitted to be worn at any given time and the collar should hang at equal distances at both the front and back.

When the collar from which the Order badge is suspended is worn, the broad (sash) riband of the same Order is not worn although it may be replaced by the broad (sash) riband and badge of another Order which the individual is entitled to wear.

In the following cases only one Order badge is provided so that when the collar is worn, the Order badge is removed from its riband and attached to the collar:-

Most Distinguished Order of St. Michael and St. George
The Royal Victorian Order
The Most Excellent Order of The British Empire

Occasions when collars may be worn are as follows:-

Easter Sunday
Ascension Day
Whit Sunday
Trinity Sunday

1st January	—	New Years Day
6th January	—	The Epiphany
25th January	—	Conversion of St. Paul
2nd February	—	Presentation of Christ at the Temple
6th February	—	Queen Elizabeth II's Accession
1st March	—	St. David's Day
17th March	—	St. Patrick's Day
25th March	—	Lady Day
21st April	—	Queen Elizabeth II's Birthday
23rd April	—	St. George's Day
29th May	—	Restoration of The Royal Family
2nd June	—	Coronation of Queen Elizabeth II
10th June	—	Duke of Edinburgh's Birthday
24th June	—	St. John the Baptist
4th August	—	Queen Elizabeth, the Queen Mother's Birthday
6th August	—	Transfiguration
29th September	—	St. Michael and All Angels
1st November	—	All Saints Day
30th November	—	St. Andrew's Day
25th December	—	Christmas Day
26th December	—	St. Stephen's Day
28th December	—	Innocents Day

In addition to the above dates, collars should be worn when the Sovereign opens or prorogues Parliament, and by those taking part in the ceremony or introduction of a Peer to the House of Lords.

Collars should be worn on the outside of mantles of chivalry and Peer's robes, and fastened by white satin bows which are 1½in. in width.

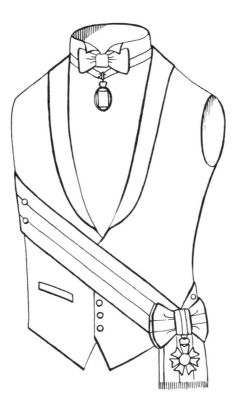

Evening Broad (sash) Riband

7. Broad (sash) Riband

Broad (sash) ribands are worn on full ceremonial occasions by Knights of The Most Noble Order of The Garter, Knights of The Most Ancient and Most Noble Order of The Thistle, Knights Grand Cross and Knights Grand Commanders. The width of the riband will vary between 3¾in. and 4in. (see page 61). The broad (sash) riband is worn over the right shoulder (with the exception of The Most Noble Order of The Garter and The Most Ancient and Most Noble Order of The Thistle, which are worn over the left shoulder), and lies diagonally across the chest with the bow from which the Order badge is suspended resting on the appropriate hip.

The Order badge may never be worn as a neck decoration, but on full ceremonial occasions when collars are worn the Order badge is transferred from the broad (sash) riband to the collar, again the exceptions are The Most Noble Order of The Garter and The Most Ancient and Most Noble Order of The Thistle, together with The Most Honourable Order of The Bath and The Most Exalted Order of The Star of India. In these cases, the Order badges are permanently fixed to the collars. All other Order badges are detached from the bow of the broad (sash) riband and attached to the collar.

At evening functions, men wear a shortened version of the broad (sash) riband. This is worn under the jacket but over the waistcoat or cummerbund. It does not pass over the shoulder and down the back like the full dress broad (sash) riband, but it is fastened to the waistcoat at the front of the armhole, with two holes and buttons, and at the opposite hip front by a pointed flap with buttonholes (see page 19).

8. Breast Stars

The breast stars of all the British Orders and most of the Foreign Orders are worn on the left hand side of the coat. The maximum number of stars that may be worn at any one time is four.

Breast stars are worn in the following positions:-

Two Stars	Three Stars	Four Stars
1	1	1
2	2 3	2 3
		4

9. Neck Decorations

On all occasions when neck decorations of an Order are worn, the full size decoration is always worn round the neck. The miniature decoration of the Order is never worn round the neck.

Only one decoration may be worn at any one time, with the decoration being suspended from a miniature width riband on all occasions. The only time when the full size riband is worn is on the occasion of the investiture of the award.

10. Official Officers of the Order

The Queen appoints Officers to the Orders of Knighthood, who look after the administrative affairs of their particular Order. Officers that are appointed do not necessarily have to be of any particular class of the Order, in fact it is not uncommon for an Officer not to be a member of the Order of which they represent.

As Badges of Office are not listed in the official Order of Precedence issued by The Central Chancery, a certain amount of confusion has arisen as to when they are to be worn. Generally speaking the Badge of Office is only worn at ceremonies held by the Order in question, these being known as Service Days.

The main problem arises however, when the Officer is a civilian and is entitled to wear an additional neck decoration. It has been suggested that on occasions deemed appropriate by the Officer, that his Badge of Office be worn in place of any other neck decoration received.

THE WEARING OF ORDERS, DECORATIONS AND MEDALS BY LADIES WITH BOTH CIVILIAN AND SERVICE FORMS OF DRESS

1. Introduction

Orders, Decorations and Medals being worn by ladies in service uniform are to be worn in exactly the same way as prescribed for men, ie Companions Badges are to be worn suspended from a miniature width riband round the neck and underneath any shirt collar. The exceptions to this rule however are female Naval Officers when their uniform incorporates a cape or bolero. In this instance the Companion class of the Order would be suspended from a bow and tails mounting, any medals being mounted from a medal brooch may be moved upwards to accommodate this Order.

2. Bow and Tails

Orders, Decorations and Medals when awarded to ladies whether military or civilian will be suspended from what is known as a bow and tails mounting (see below). However, if the Order, Decoration or Medal is to be worn whilst in service dress then the Order, Decoration or Medal must be removed from the bow and tails mounting and converted to the gentleman's style of wearing as detailed above in the introduction.

Only one bow and tails mounted Order, Decoration or Medal may be worn on the same occasion. In the case of Commander/Companion class and above the most senior Order or most appropriate Order for the occasion would be worn. However for classes below and other Decorations and Medals two or more may be worn together but they would have to be mounted together on a pin brooch as if for a gentleman.

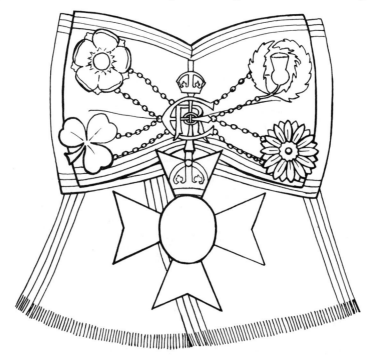

The Royal Victorian Chain as worn by a lady

The same rules apply with miniature Orders, Decorations and Medals, that is, if only one is worn it may be suspended from a bow and tails mounting, but if two or more are to be worn then they must be mounted from a pin brooch as if for a gentleman.

Evening Dress

3. Evening Dress

Dames Grand Cross—One broad (sash) riband, of the senior British Order, is worn with its badge unless it is deemed appropriate for a junior British or Foreign Order to be worn in its place. Up to four breast stars (of various classes) may be worn on the left side of the dress. If one star only is worn, it is to be placed approximately 6in. above the waist. However, if there is more than one star to be accommodated, then they are worn in the same manner as by a gentleman, with the lowest star being positioned 6in. above the waist (see page 20).

Dames Commander—Up to four breast stars (of various classes) may be worn on the left side of the dress. If only one star is to be worn, it is to be placed 6in. above the waist, but if there are more than one, then they are to be arranged as if to be worn by a gentleman, with the lowest star being positioned 6in. above the waist (see page 20).

The full size decoration is worn on a full size bow and tails mounting and is suspended above the breast stars. Any other miniature medals mounted on a brooch are worn in addition and are positioned above the decoration. The maximum number of badges on a bow and tails mounting is one.

Companions and Commanders—The full size decoration is worn suspended from a bow and tails mounting, on the left side of the dress. The maximum number that can be worn at any time is one. Miniature medals being worn on a brooch are to be positioned above the decoration. A miniature of the Order may only be worn if the recipient is wearing other miniature medals on a brooch, and another full size Order is being worn.

Lieutenants, Officers and Members—The badge is worn in miniature on the left side of the dress. If worn on its own it should have a bow and tails mounting. However, if the recipient is entitled to wear more than one miniature Order, Decoration or Medal, then they are all to be mounted together on one brooch in the same fashion as if to be worn by a gentleman. If worn singly, the full size badge may be worn alone.

Order of Merit, Companion of Honour, Crown of India—These Orders are worn on the left side of the dress, suspended from a bow and tails mounting, and are positioned below any miniature medals being worn. They are never worn in miniature form, and the maximum number to be worn at any time is one. However, if the holder is entitled to other medals the Crown of India may be mounted on a brooch and worn on the left side as by a gentleman.

Royal Victorian Chain—When worn by ladies, the chain is attached to the bow and tails of the riband of the Victorian Order this being worn in the left side below any miniature medals. It is never worn in miniature form (see page 22).

4. Official Day Functions

Dames Grand Cross—A maximum of four breast stars may be worn, positioned on the left side, with the only or lowest star being positioned six inches above the waist. Two or more stars are worn in the same manner as if for a gentleman. The broad (sash) riband and Order badge are not worn. Collars are only worn if ordered for a special occasion.

Dames Commander—A maximum of four breast stars may be worn as described above, but the Order badge is not worn.

Commanders, Order of Merit, Companion of Honour—The full size ladies decoration is worn suspended from a bow and tails mounting on the left side below any medals mounted on a brooch. Only one decoration may be worn at any one time.

Lieutenants, Officers, Members, Crown of India—When worn singly the full size Order is worn suspended from a bow and tails mounting on the left side. However, if the holder is entitled to other medals, it should be mounted on a brooch and worn on the left side, as by a gentleman.

Royal Victorian Chain
When worn by ladies, the chain is attached to a bow and tails mounting on the riband of the Royal Victorian Order. This Order is worn on the left side below any medal bar.

5. Collars

Collars of the Orders of Knighthood are worn by Ladies of The Most Noble Order of The Garter and Ladies of The Most Ancient and Most Noble Order of The Thistle, Dames Grand Cross at appropriate ceremonies and other full ceremonial occasions when due notification has been given, they are never worn after sunset.

Only one collar is permitted to be worn at any one time and the collar should hang at equal lengths at both the front and the back. When the collar from which the Order badge is suspended, is worn, the broad (sash) riband of the same Order is not worn although it may be replaced by the broad (sash) riband and badge of another Order which the individual is entitled to wear.

In the following cases only one order badge is provided so that when the collar is worn, the broad (sash) riband Order badge is removed from its riband and attached to the collar:-
Most Distinguished Order of St. Michael and St. George
The Royal Victorian Order
The Most Excellent Order of The British Empire

Occasions when collars may be worn are as follows:-
Easter Sunday
Ascension Day
Whit Sunday
Trinity Sunday

1st January	—	New Years Day
6th January	—	The Epiphany
25th January	—	Conversion of St. Paul
2nd February	—	Presentation of Christ in the Temple
6th February	—	Queen Elizabeth II's Accession
1st March	—	St. David's Day
17th March	—	St. Patrick's Day
25th March	—	Lady Day
21st April	—	Queen Elizabeth II's Birthday
23rd April	—	St. George's Day
29th May	—	Restoration of The Royal Family
2nd June	—	Coronation of Queen Elizabeth II
10th June	—	Duke of Edinburgh's Birthday
24th June	—	St. John the Baptist
4th August	—	Queen Elizabeth, the Queen Mother's Birthday
6th August	—	Transfiguration
29th September	—	St. Michael and All Angels
1st November	—	All Saints Day
30th November	—	St. Andrew's Day
25th December	—	Christmas Day
26th December	—	St Stephen's Day
28th December	—	Innocents Day

In addition to the above dates, collars should be worn when Her Majesty opens or prorogues Parliament, and by those taking part in the ceremony or introduction of a Peer to the House of Lords.

Collars should be worn on the outside of mantles of chivalry and Peer's robes, and fastened by white satin bows which are 1½in. in width.

6. Broad (sash) Ribands

Broad (sash) ribands are worn on full ceremonial occasions by Ladies of The Most Noble Order of The Garter, Ladies of The Most Ancient and Most Noble Order of The Thistle, and Dames Grand Cross. The width of the broad (sash) riband is 2¼in. with the exceptions being The Most Noble Order of The Garter and The Most Ancient and Most Noble Order of The Thistle, which are the same width as for gentlemen, ie 4in.

On all occasions when the broad (sash) riband is worn, ladies wear it passing over the appropriate shoulder with the bow normally being attached to the dress to prevent any movement.

The Order badge may never be worn as a neck decoration, but on full ceremonial occasions when collars are to be worn, the Order badge is suspended from the collar. Again the exceptions to this are The Most Noble Order of The Garter and The Most Ancient and Most Noble Order of The Thistle, together with The Most Honorable Order of The Bath. In these cases, the Order badges are permanently fixed to the collar. All other badges are detached from the bow of the broad (sash) riband and attached to the collar.

7. Breast Stars

The breast stars of all British Orders, and most foreign Orders, are worn on the left side of the dress, coat or tunic. The maximum number of breast stars that may be worn at any time is four. This includes any breast stars given by foreign countries, in which the recipient has received the Queen's permission to wear. A recipient who has been awarded more than one breast star from the same country will wear only one—usually the first one to be awarded, unless the later ones are of a higher class or are of a more senior Order.

Day uniform
A)   If only one star is to be worn, it should be placed in the centre of the breast pocket, the upper point being not less than 1in. below the lip of the pocket, or in the corresponding position on a garment without a breast pocket.
B)   If two stars are worn, the second star is placed directly below the first, with its upper point not less than 1in. below the lowest point of the first star.
C)   When three stars are worn, they should be positioned in a triangular formation with stars two and three in a horizontal line below the first star. The second star is worn innermost on the chest.
D)   On occasions where the above interferes with the broad (sash) riband the second star can be worn alongside the first star, with the latter innermost on the chest and the third star below.

E)   When four stars are worn, they are arranged in a diamond formation, the first, second and third stars being worn as indicated above.

Two Stars	Three Stars	Four Stars
1	1	1
2	2 3	2 3
		4

When either three or four stars are worn, it is necessary to position the first so that the second is clear at the top left hand button of the coat. For this purpose it is permissible for the top breast star to be worn with the upper point up to ½in. above the lip of the breast pocket.

Unless unrestricted permission has been granted, breast stars that have been awarded by a foreign country can only be worn if the recipient is attending a function hosted by that particular country. In this case, the foreign stars take precedence over any British breast stars that are being worn. (See pages 53-56).

Evening Wear and Mess Dress

On the occasions when breast stars are to be worn with evening and mess dress, they are to be worn in the same manner as when wearing uniform. However, it is advised that beckets are attached to the coat. A maximum number of four stars may be worn, this including any foreign stars permitted to be worn.

The positioning of the breast stars is as follows:-

One Star   — centrally covering the middle button.

Two Stars   — one above the other, the senior between the top and middle buttons, the junior between the middle and bottom buttons.

Three Stars — a triangular formation, the senior Order between the top and middle buttons with the second and third breast stars alongside each other between the middle and bottom buttons.

Four Stars — in a diamond formation. (see above).

When Officers dress includes a cape or bolero, the breast stars are to be worn on the cape or bolero and not on the dress. If a single star is worn, it should be placed centrally 6in. above the waist on the left side. Any additional stars are to be worn in the same manner as when worn by men, with the lowest star 6in. above the waist.

8. H.M. Diplomatic Service

The regulations for the wearing of Orders, Decorations and Medals are exactly the same as previously mentioned for ladies.

The Diplomatic Service Badge however is only worn by a lady in a position in which her male counterpart is entitled to wear a diplomatic uniform, and should be worn suspended from a dark blue bow on the left side underneath any other medals that are to be worn.

ARMED FORCES
AND UNIFORMED PERSONNEL

1. Collars
2. Broad (sash) Ribands
3. Breast Stars
4. Neck Decorations
5. Awards prior to enlistment
6. Official Officers of the Orders of Knighthood
7. H.M. Diplomatic Service

30

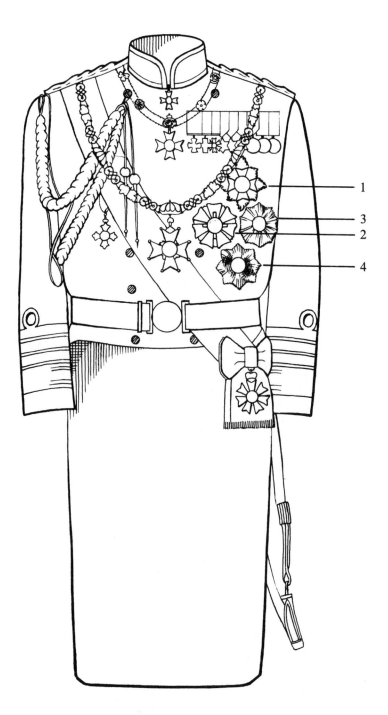

1

3
2

4

Naval Ceremonial Day Coat

1. Collars

Collars of the Orders of Knighthood are worn by Knights of The Most Noble Order of The Garter, Knights of The Most Ancient and Most Noble Order of The Thistle, Knights Grand Cross at appropriate ceremonies and other full ceremonial occasions when due notification has been given. They are not to be worn after sunset, nor when mounted on ceremonial parades such as the Trooping the Colour.

Only one collar is permitted to be worn at any given time, and they pass under the shoulder boards or epaulettes near the outer edge, but over any aiguillettes when in uniform. The collar should hang at an equal distance at both the front and the back.

When the collar (from which the Order badge is suspended) is worn, the broad (sash) riband of the same Order is not worn, although it may be replaced by the broad (sash) riband and badge of another Order which the individual is entitled to wear.

In the following cases, only one Order badge is provided so that when the collar is worn, the Order badge is removed from its riband and attached to the collar:-

Most Distinguished Order of St. Michael and St. George
The Royal Victorian Order
The Most Excellent Order of The British Empire

Occasions when collars may be worn are as follows:-

Easter Sunday		
Ascension Day		
Whit Sunday		
Trinity Sunday		
1st January	—	New Years Day
6th January	—	The Epiphany
25th January	—	Conversion of St. Paul
2nd February	—	Presentation of Christ at the Temple
6th February	—	Queen Elizabeth II's Accession
1st March	—	St. David's Day
17th March	—	St. Patrick's Day
25th March	—	Lady Day
21st April	—	Queen Elizabeth II's Birthday
23rd April	—	St. George's Day
29th May	—	Restoration of The Royal Family
2nd June	—	Coronation of Queen Elizabeth II
10th June	—	Duke of Edinburgh's Birthday
24th June	—	St. John the Baptist
4th August	—	Queen Elizabeth, the Queen Mother's Birthday
6th August	—	Transfiguration
29th September	—	St. Michael and All Angels
1st November	—	All Saints Day
30th November	—	St. Andrew's Day
25th December	—	Christmas Day
26th December	—	St. Stephen's Day
28th December	—	Innocents Day

In addition to the above dates, collars should be worn when the Her Majesty opens or prorogues Parliament, and by those taking part in the ceremony or introduction of a Peer to the House of Lords.

Collars should be worn on the outside of mantles of chivalry and Peer's robes, and fastened by white satin bows which are 1½in. in width.

2. Broad (sash) Ribands

Broad (sash) ribands are worn on full ceremonial occasions by gentlemen who are Knights of The Most Noble Order of The Garter, Knights of The Most Ancient and Most Noble Order of The Thistle and Knights Grand Cross.

The width of broad (sash) ribands for gentlemen will vary depending on the particular Order, being between 3¾in. and 4in. The broad (sash) riband is worn over the right shoulder (with the exception of The Most Noble Order of The Garter and The Most Ancient and Most Noble Order of The Thistle, which are worn over the left shoulder), and lies diagonally across the chest with the bow from which the Order badge is suspended resting on the appropriate hip. The broad (sash) riband should be worn under any strap or aiguillette. Any waist belt should pass over the broad (sash) riband.

Order badges may never be worn as neck decorations, but on full ceremonial occasions when collars are worn, the Order badge is suspended from the collar. Again, the exceptions to this are The Most Noble Order of The Garter and The Most Ancient and Most Noble Order of The Thistle together with The Most Honourable Order of The Bath. In these cases, the Order badges are permanently fixed to the collar. All other Order badges are detached from the bow of the broad (sash) riband and attached to the collar.

At evening functions, when wearing evening or mess dress, men wear shortened versions of the broad (sash) riband. This is worn under the jacket but over the waistcoat or cummerbund. It does not pass over the shoulder and down the back like the full dress broad (sash) riband, but is to be fastened to the waistcoat at the front of the armhole, with two holes and buttons, and at the opposite hip front by a pointed flap with buttonholes. See page 19.

3. Breast Stars

The breast stars of all British Orders, and most Foreign Orders, are worn on the left side of the coat or tunic. The maximum number of breast stars to be worn at any one time is four. This includes any breast stars given by a Foreign country and for which the recipient has the Queen's permission to wear. However, R.A.F. regulations state that not more than on Foreign breast star may ever be worn with uniform on any occasion. A holder of more than on Foreign star from the same country is normally to wear that which has been awarded first.

R.A.F. No. 1 Dress

Day Uniform

(A) If only one star is to be worn, it should be placed in the centre of the breast pocket, the upper point being not less than 1in. below the lip of the pocket, or in the corresponding position on a garment without a breast pocket.

(B) If two stars are to be worn, the second star is placed directly below the first, with its upper point not less then 1in. below the lowest point of the first star.

(C) When three stars are worn, they should be positioned in a triangular formation with stars two and three in a horizontal line below the first star. The second star is worn innermost on the chest.

(D) On occasions when the above interferes with the broad (sash) riband the second star can be worn alongside the first, with the latter innermost on the chest and the third star below.

(E) When four stars are to be worn, they are arranged in a diamond formation, the first, second and third stars being worn as indicated above, with the fourth below.

Two Stars	*Three Stars*	*Four Stars*
1	1	1
2	2 3	2 3
		4

When either three or four stars are worn, it is necessary to position the first so that the second is clear at the top left hand button of the coat. For this purpose it is permissible for the top breast star to be worn with its upper point up to ½in. above the lip of the breast pocket.

Unless unrestricted permission has been granted, breast stars that have been awarded by a foreign country can only be worn if the recipient is attending a function hosted by that particular country. In this case, the foreign stars take precedence over any British breast stars that are being worn.

Evening Wear (Mess Dress)

On the occasions when breast stars are to be worn with evening and mess dress, they are to be worn in the same manner as when wearing uniform. However it is advised that beckets are attached to the coat. A maximum number of four breast stars may be worn, this including any foreign breast stars permitted to be worn.

The positioning of the breast stars is as follows:-

One Star — centrally covering the middle button.

Two Stars — one above the other, the senior between the top and middle buttons, the junior between the middle and bottom buttons.

Three Stars — a triangular formation, the senior Order between the top and middle buttons with the second and third stars alongside each other between the middle and bottom buttons.

Four Stars — in a diamond formation (see diagram above).

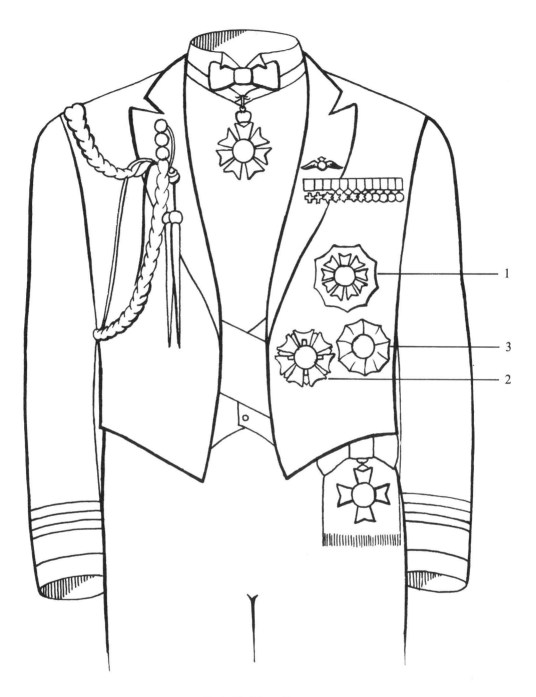

R.A.F. Mess Dress

4. Neck Decorations

On all occasions when neck decorations of an Order are worn, the full size decoration is always worn round the neck. The miniature badge is never worn round the neck.

Naval

On ceremonial coats with a stand collar and Royal Marine tunics, the first or only neck decoration is worn on a miniature width riband. This is worn inside the coat or tunic with the neck decoration emerging between the hook and eye and the bottom of the collar to hang ¾in. below the collar. If a second decoration is worn it is suspended from a small eye stitched inside the coat or tunic on a 3in. length of miniature riband emerging from between the first and second buttons on the right hand side of the coat or tunic.

When a turn down collar and tie are to be worn, the first or only neck decoration is again worn on a miniature width riband. This is worn inside the collar and over the tie, being suspended immediately below the position of the knot of the tie. The second decoration is worn immediatly below the first and rests on the cross of the lapel, the decoration itself being suspended from a length of riband fastened by a hook onto the inside of the shirt.

Army

The maximum number of neck decorations permitted to be worn is three, with the most senior being worn round the neck. The decoration is suspended from a miniature width riband (except when wearing No. 2 or No. 4 dress when Army Dress Regulation 825 states that the riband of a Companion or Membership width is worn). The riband is worn under the collar and emerges to hang ¾in. below the collar, just below the knot of the tie.

A second neck decoration may be worn below the first suspended from a riband tunic slip emerging ¾in. below the top buttonhole of the jacket, the riband being secured by a hook. The third decoration should emerge from the second button in the same manner. In both cases, a small eye is stitched to the inside of the jacket or tunic.

R.A.F.

The maximum number of neck decorations that are permitted to be worn are as follows:-
Two for ceremonial dress (full)
One for ceremonial dress (normal)
This includes any foreign Orders that may have been awarded.

The decoration is worn on a miniature width riband under the collar so that it hangs at a length of ¾in. just below the knot of the tie. This applies to the senior Order. The second decoration emerges to hang ¾in. below the top buttonhole. A small eye is stitched to the inside of the jacket or tunic by the buttonhole to which the riband is fastened by means of a hook.

All Services

At evening functions only one neck decoration is permitted to be worn, this is suspended from a miniature width riband with a wing collar and bow tie, outside the collar but underneath the tie, with the decoration hanging as close as possible to the bow.

With the exception of the Army, the neck decoration of an Order is always suspended from a miniature width riband, otherwise, the only time that a full size neck riband is worn is at the investiture of the Order.

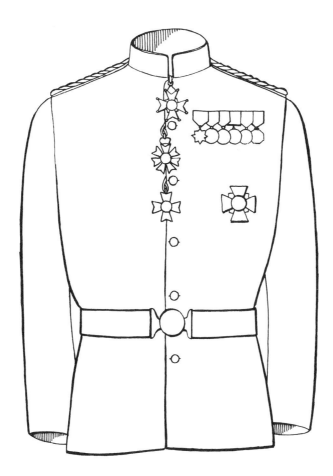

Maximum number of neck decorations to be worn
by the Army

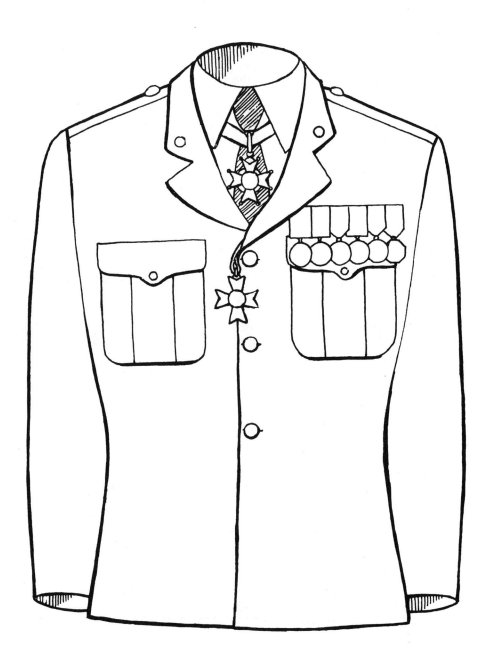

Method of wearing 2 neck decorations
with service dress

5. Awards prior to enlistment

Any individual who has been awarded, prior to enlistment, any Order, Decoration or Medal that is listed in the Order of Precedence, including any foreign Orders, Decorations and Medals authorised for wear and awarded by the Sovereign, is entitled to wear their award, irrespective of status at the time. For example, someone winning the Queen's Gallantry Medal would be entitled to wear this award if they subsequently enlisted in one of the services.

6. Official Officers of the Orders of Knighthood

The Queen appoints Officers to the Orders of Knighthood who look after the administrative affairs of their particular Order. Officers that are appointed do not necessarily have to be of any particular class within the Order, in fact it is not uncommon for an Officer not to be a member of the Order they represent. As Badges of Office are not listed in the official Order of Precedence issued by The Central Chancery a certain amount of confusion had arisen as to when they are to be worn. Generally speaking the Badge of Office is only worn at ceremonies held by the Order in question, these being known as Service Days.

The Badge of Office may be worn as one of the neck decorations permitted to be worn as stipulated in the wearers service regulations and not in addition to the maximum number of neck decorations permitted.

7. H.M. Diplomatic Service

The regulations for the wearing of Orders, Decorations and Medals with diplomatic uniform are, that a maximum of four breast stars may be worn at any one time. They are worn in the diamond formation as previously discussed and the maximum number of neck decorations to be worn is three. The riband of the senior decoration is worn inside the collar of the uniform. Subsequent decorations are worn immediately below with the riband of the second emerging between the second and third buttons of the coat and the riband of the third emerging from between the third and fourth buttons. For this purpose, small eyes should be stitched inside the coat to which the ribands may be fastened by hooks.

FULL SIZE MEDALS
MOUNTED FOR WEAR

42

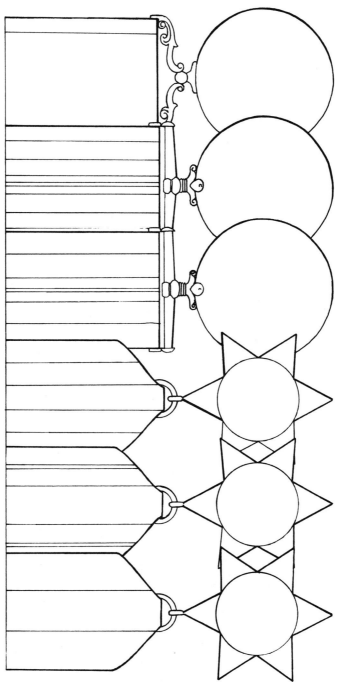

Medals mounted ordinary style (obverse)

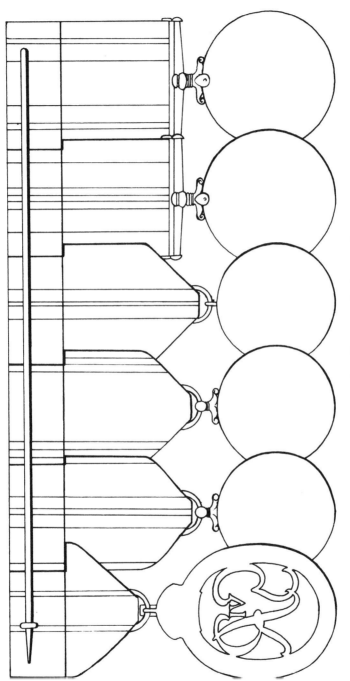

Medals mounted ordinary style (reverse)

43

1. Introduction

Orders, Decorations and Medals which are normally worn on the left breast should be worn in a horizontal line and be suspended from a single brooch of which no part should be seen. The most senior medal according to the Order of Precedence (see page 1) is positioned furthest from the left shoulder. The maximum number of Orders, Decorations and Medals that are permitted to be worn side by side is five. However, when they cannot be suspended in this manner, on account of their number, they are overlapped (see page 42). It should be noted that the first medal and riband must be completely seen.

Medals should be worn in such a manner as to show the obverse to the front which is usually the Sovereign's Head, Coat of Arms, Flag or Cypher.

The length of the riband is to be 1¼in. from the top of the riband to the top of the suspension or first clasp, shorter ribands should not be worn. If there are two or more medals they should be arranged so that the bottom rim or point of the medals are in line. Owing to the different sizes of Orders, Decorations and Medals it may be necessary to wear the ribands longer than 1¼in.

A length of riband is to be worn in respect of any Order, Decoration or Medal awarded but not yet received, but only when others already received are required to be worn. This riband would normally be the same length as the preceding one.

As an alternative to awards hanging loosely from their ribands, Orders, Decorations and Medals may be mounted in the royal (or court) style, i.e. insignia mounted on a cloth and buckram covered metal frame, the length of which will depend on the length of the first Order, Decoration or Medal which is to be mounted (see page 46).

The frame must show 1¼in. of riband from its top to the suspension ring, bar or clasp of the Order, Decoration or Medal. The riband is then extended over the back of the frame and up the front so that it covers the frame behind the insignia.

The Orders, Decorations and Medals are sewn to the frame and should reach approximately to the centre behind the Orders, Decorations and Medals, but they must all be level at the bottom edge. After 5 medals it is then usual for them to begin to overlap (see Navy, below).

The main advantage of this style over the ordinary style mounting is that the insignia are firmly fixed and the risk of damage to any enamelled or polished surface from abrasion is reduced.

2. Navy

Medals awarded to Naval personnel are worn in the same manner as previously outlined, but dress regulations differ as follows:-
a) medals should overlap when three or more are worn in the case of Ratings and ranks below Officer.
b) the riband length should be 1¾in. from the top of the riband to the ring, suspension bar or first named clasp on the first medal, thereafter the other medals may be adjusted accordingly so that the lowest part of each medal is in line. The minimum amount of riband to be showing is ½in. above the top clasp as in the case of a multiple bar General Service Medal.
c) medals are to be worn ordinary style unless there are sufficient number to warrant overlapping in which case they may be worn royal (or court) style by Officers only.

In all cases, the medals must be worn so as to hide any ribands sewn onto uniform which are being worn by means of a felt flap attached to the medal bar and falling down behind the ribands and medals.

3. Medals worn on the right breast

The Sovereign's permission has been granted for the medals listed below to be worn on the right breast of the recipients.
Royal Humane Society Medals
Stanhope Gold Medal
Royal National Lifeboat Institution Medal
Order of St. John of Jerusalem Life Saving Medal

4. Emblems worn on full size medal ribands

There are a variety of reasons why additional 'clasps' or 'bars' are attached to medal ribands.
A) To denote a second award of a gallantry or long service medal. This is so that the recipient need not wear more than one example of the same decoration or medal.
B) On occasions where it is deemed appropriate for one campaign service medal to be awarded for multiple campaigns dated or named clasps are awarded, for example the current General Service Medal which can carry multiple clasps to denote service in more than one action/area.
C) In 1919 the King approved that a dated clasp '5th Aug.-22nd Nov. 1914' be awarded to recipients of the 1914 Star who served under fire of the enemy in France and Belgium during those dates.
D) The practice of awarding clasps on campaign stars continued in the Second World War with clasps being awarded to go on certain campaign medals rather than the recipients being awarded a second campaign star.

Medal	Clasp awarded
1939/45 Star	Battle of Britain
Atlantic Star	Air crew Europe or France and Germany
Air Crew Europe Star	Atlantic or France and Germany
Africa Star	8th Army, 1st Army or North Africa 1942/43
Pacific Star	Burma
Burma Star	Pacific
France and Germany Star	Atlantic

The maximum number of clasps that are permitted to be worn on one campaign star of World War II is one.

46

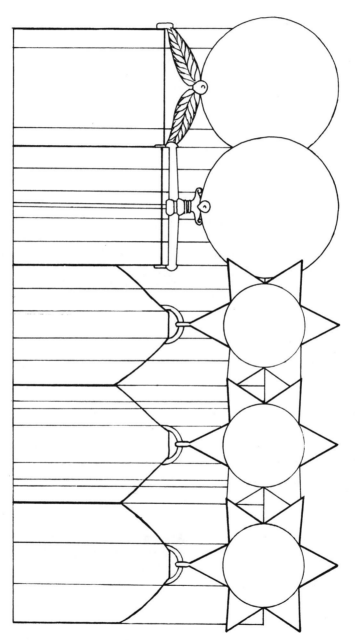

Medals mounted royal (or court) style (obverse)

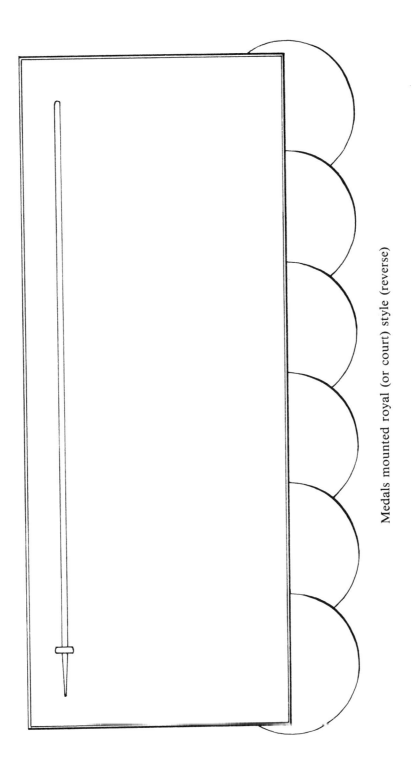

Medals mounted royal (or court) style (reverse)

5. Rosettes

In the case of Foreign Orders, rosettes can be worn to denote the class of the Order. In addition to the rosettes being worn on the riband, an example of the rosette may also be worn in the buttonhole while the wearer is in everyday civilian dress.

A rosette worn on the full size medal will denote that the Order is a 4th class award as opposed to the 5th class award as more often than not the actual badge will be the same size and design.

6. Mention in Despatches

In 1920 King George V approved that an emblem should be worn on the WWI Victory Medal riband to denote a person being mentioned in wartime despatches. The emblem was to take the form of a multiple leaved bronze oak leaf. Only one emblem was to be worn, irrespective of the number of times any individual had been mentioned.

Mention in Despatches 1914-1919
The emblem of bronze oak leaves is worn on the riband of the Victory Medal. The award of this emblem ceased as from 10 August 1920.

Mention in Despatches 1920-1939
The single bronze oak leaf emblem, if granted for service in operations between the two World Wars, is worn on the riband of the appropriate General Service Medal. If a G.S.M. has not been granted, the emblem is worn directly on the coat after any medal ribands. If there are no ribands, it is worn in the position of a single riband.

Mention in Despatches 1939-1945
This single leaved emblem is to be worn on the 1939-45 War Medal, or if this has not been awarded, directly after any medal ribands.

Mention in Despatches subsequent to 1945
The single bronze oak leaf is to be worn on the relevant campaign medal above any clasp. If a medal has not been granted then it is worn directly on the coat after any medal ribands. If there are no ribands, it is worn in the position of a single riband. It should be placed above any clasp or emblem or rosette which is also permitted to be worn on the relevant medal riband.

Mention in Despatches emblems are worn on the riband of the full size medal at an angle of 60° from the inside edge of the riband, the leaves should point upwards towards the left shoulder with the stalk at the lowest point. If the emblem is not worn with a campaign medal, it can be worn after any Order, Decoration or Medal on a piece of cloth covered buckram.

The single bronze oak leaf emblem was also granted from the end of the 1939-45 War up to 1952 to denote a Queen's Commendation for Brave Conduct, and a Queen's Commendation for Valuable Services in the Air.

7. South Atlantic Medal

A Mention in Despatches emblem that has been awarded should be worn above the rosette (if applicable), and placed at an angle of 60° with the leaves pointing upwards to the left shoulder.

8. King/Queen's Commendation for Brave Conduct

Since 1952 a silver laurel leaved emblem has been granted to civilians only, other than those in the merchant navy. During World War II this emblem was worn on the Defence Medal if appropriate or it was worn after any medals, or, if no medals had been awarded to the recipient, it was worn in the place of a single medal.

9. Queen's Commendation for Valuable Services in the Air

This award was instituted in 1942 in recognition for gallantry not reaching the required standard to be awarded the Air Force Cross. The badge, a silver oval, is worn on the coat immediately below any medals or ribands. In civilian air line uniform, it is worn on the panel of the left breast pocket.

10. Wearing of Medals by Next of Kin

A misunderstanding often arises over the wearing of medals by the widow or heir of a deceased person on such occasions as Armistice parades.

There are no statutes or regulations to support this idea, but over the years it has become generally accepted that if the medals are worn then they should be worn on the right hand side of the coat or jacket.

MINIATURE MEDALS

These are exact replicas of their equivalent full size badges and according to the ruling made by King George V in 1923 are to be approximately half the size of the equivalent full size piece. As far as the miniatures of Orders are concerned, they are to be half the size of the lowest class of the full size Order.

The following British Orders and Decorations are not worn in the miniature size:-
The Most Noble Order of The Garter
The Most Ancient and Most Noble Order of The Thistle
The Order of Merit
The Imperial Order of The Crown of India
The Order of The Companions of Honour
Baronet's Badge

Miniatures of all Orders, Decorations and Medals (with the exception of the above) are worn only at evening functions. Foreign awards are worn subject to the rules governing permission to wear, being restricted or unrestricted. (See pages 55-56).

It is not permissible to wear a single miniature of an Order if the full size version is being worn, for example, a C.B.E. neck badge and C.B.E. miniature worn singly. However, an example of the miniature Order may be worn if the recipient is wearing two or more Orders, Decorations or Medals in miniature form, suspended on a medal brooch.

All miniature Orders, Decorations and Medals to which the wearer is entitled, should be mounted together on a medal brooch. The overall depth of the miniature medal and riband is 2in. from the top of the riband to the bottom point of the medal unless the unusual shape or size of the medal dictates otherwise.

Royal Household
Some liveried members of the Royal Household wear full size or miniature medals mounted in the royal (or court) style while on duty.

THE WEARING OF FOREIGN ORDERS, DECORATIONS AND MEDALS INCLUDING COMMONWEALTH COUNTRIES OF WHICH THE QUEEN IS NOT THE HEAD OF STATE

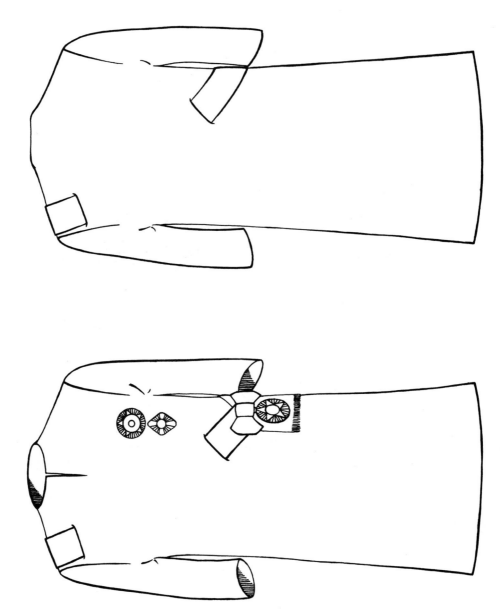

Suggested form of Arab dress to incorporate broad (sash) riband

1. Introduction

The Queen's subjects are not permitted to accept and wear the insignia of an Order or Decoration of a Foreign country or of a Commonwealth country of which the Queen is not the Head of State, unless permission has been granted by the Sovereign. This permission is granted on application to the Secretary of State for Foreign and Commonwealth Affairs with whom the proposal will normally have been cleared in advance, through the diplomatic channels of the government making the award. Permission is granted in one of two ways, namely restricted or unrestricted.

2. Restricted

In this instance, the recipient receives instructions from the Sovereign's Private Secretary regarding the occasions when the insignia may be worn:-

(a) in the presence of the Sovereign, Prince or Head of State to which the Order, Decoration or Medal belongs.
(b) in the presence of any member of the Royal Family of the country concerned.
(c) at the residence of any Ambassadors, High Commissioners, Ministers or Consular Officers of that country, either in the United Kingdom or overseas.
(d) when attached to, or when officially meeting any Ministers or Officers of the Army, Navy or Air Force, or any official deputation of the country concerned.
(e) at any official or semi-official ceremony held exclusively in connection with the country concerned—a memorial service, the unveiling of a monument, or the opening of an official institution.
(f) on all official occasions whilst in that country, when a person is attending one of the above functions, any Order belonging to that particular country should take precedence over any British Order that the recipient may be entitled to wear. For example, when the Foreign Order consists of a neck decoration and breast star, this should be worn in place of the British Order.

Decorations and medals of the country that is hosting the function and that are normally worn mounted from a medal bar, should be worn hanging centrally over the full size or miniature medal bar. It is generally accepted that if any members of the armed forces who are serving for an extended period of time in an overseas force and receive Orders, Decorations and Medals from the particular country where they are serving, then those items should take precedence over any British Orders, Decorations and Medals while serving in that country or subsequently, on any occasion connected with that country.

3. Unrestricted Permission

This enables Foreign insignia to be worn on all occasions when any British insignia is worn so that, decorations and medals which are usually worn from a medal brooch may be mounted permanently after any British Orders, Decorations and Medals. Their order should be based on that listed in the Order of Precedence, i.e. Orders then Decorations then Medals in order of date award.

It is generally accepted that if any members of the armed forces who are serving for an extended period of time in an overseas force and receive Orders, Decorations and Medals from that particular country where they are serving, then those items should take precedence over any British Orders, Decorations and Medals while serving in that country or subsequently, on any occasion connected with that country.

THE WEARING OF RIBANDS ONLY

1. Introduction

Riband bars are strips of riband only and, with the exception of ribands of medals usually worn on the right breast (such as approved Life Saving Awards, etc. issued by private societies), are worn on the left breast when the wearer is in uniform or on any occasion when in civilian dress. There are two types of riband bar:-

(1) where the ribands are sewn onto a metal brooch pin enabling them to be detached from the coat, or uniform
(2) where the ribands are sewn onto a strip of buckram and then stitched onto the coat or uniform.

Ribands of Orders, Decorations or Medals in which restricted permission has been granted should not be included, unless the recipient is serving in the country of award when they would usually take precedence over any British Order, Decoration or Medal. Ribands of all Orders, Decorations and Medals, with the exception of The Most Noble Order of The Garter and The Most Ancient and Most Noble Order of The Thistle, and Baronet's Badge are represented on riband bars. In the case of multiple class Orders the riband of the lowest class is worn and this will usually be between 1 ¼ in. and 1 ½ in. wide. In the case of any Foreign Orders being worn a rosette can be placed on the riband to denote the class of the Order (see page 62). Ribands are to be worn in the correct order of precedence, with the most senior riband nearest to the lapel and in the top row when more than one row is worn. The ribands are worn side by side with no gaps or overlay between each riband, and the maximum number of ribands permitted in one row is five, unless official dress regulations state otherwise.

Ribands may be worn immediately after the date on which the official notification has been received, even though the Order, Decoration or Medal itself may not have been received.

2. Navy

The depth of riband to be worn is ½ in., but when five or more rows are worn this may be reduced to ⅜ in. Royal Marines ⅜ in. in all cases. The ribands are to be sewn onto the garment on all occasions except when wearing whites, tropical khaki and stone coloured clothes when a pin-on riband bar is worn.

Officers—see diagram opposite.

Individual rows should be ¼ in. apart, but this gap may be reduced if a large number of rows are worn.

The position of the riband bar is such that the top or only row is 1in. below the point of the shoulder, any additional rows being positioned so that they are visible whilst preserving as symmetrical an arrangement as possible. However, no row should be made up so that it is longer than the one above.

Ratings—see diagram opposite.

The top or only row is worn on a level with the point of the lapel. With blue jumpers 4 ½ in. below the point of the shoulder, and with white uniform 2in. below the point of the shoulder. Unlike Officers, in the case of multiple rows, no row is to be shorter than the one above, and the whole display should be as symmetrical as possible.

Miniature width ribands

Ribands are to be ⅜ in. in depth. They can never be worn as buckram bars (sew on) and are only worn on mess dress in the same position as miniature medals.

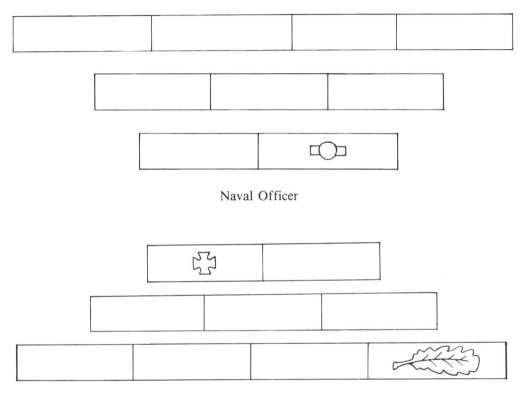

Naval Officer

Naval Rating

3. Army
(see diagram page 60)

The correct depth of a riband for the Army is ⅜ in. They are placed centrally over the left breast pocket button, as previously mentioned, and the ribands should be positioned such that none are totally or partially obscured by the lapel of the jacket. The maximum number of ribands worn in a complete row is five, and any row consisting of less than five ribands should be placed centrally over the top complete row. The edges of the ribands nearest the shoulder in each complete row must be in line vertically with the bottom row. The rows should by ⅛ in. apart, but if more than four rows are worn, there should be no space in between.

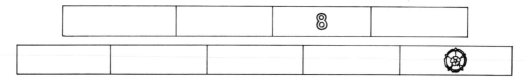

Army

4. Royal Air Force
(see diagram below)

The correct depth of riband for the R.A.F. is $\frac{7}{16}$in. (11mm.). A row should not consist of more than four ribands side by side, but when four or more ribands are worn, they should be made up to display as many complete rows of four as possible, a row consisting of less than four ribands should be placed at the top. Each succeeding row should be placed centrally above the row immediately below it, except on those occasions when it may be necessary to shorten certain rows to ensure that no riband or part of a riband is obscured by the lapel or collar of the jacket. The upper row should be shortened as necessary in order to display as many complete ribands as possible in the space between the edge of the lapel and the top of the sleeve. The edges of the riband in each complete row of four must be vertically in line with the inner edge of the bottom row. This, in turn, should be located immediately and centrally above the flap of the breast pocket, or in the appropriate position when a pocket is not fitted. The space between the rows should be $\frac{1}{8}$in. (3mm.), but if four or more rows are worn, then there should not be any space between the rows.

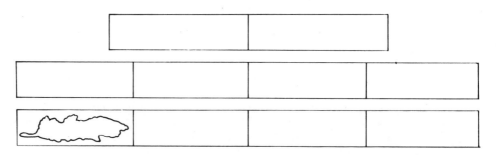

R.A.F.

5. The widths of ribands used with insignia and on riband bars

	With Insignia	On Uniform
Order of The Garter	4in.	Not worn
Order of The Thistle	4in.	Not worn
G.C.B.	4in.	1½in.
Dames Grand Cross (G.C.B.)	2¼in.	1½in.
K.C.B.	2in.	1½in.
D.C.B.	1¾in.	1½in.
C.B.	1½in.	1½in.
Order of Merit	2in.	2in.
G.C.S.I.	4in.	1½in.
K.C.S.I.	2in.	1½in.
C.S.I.	1½in.	1½in.
G.C.M.G.	4in.	1½in.
Dames Grand Cross (G.C.M.G.)	2¼in.	1½in.
K.C.M.G.	2in.	1½in.
D.C.M.G.	1¾in.	1½in.
C.M.G.	1½in.	1½in.
G.C.I.E.	4in.	1½in.
K.C.I.E.	2in.	1½in.
C.I.E.	1½in.	1½in.
G.C.V.O.	3¾in.	1¼in.
Dames Grand Cross (G.C.V.O.)	2¼in.	1¼in.
K.C.V.O.	1¾in.	1¼in.
D.C.V.O.	1¾in.	1¼in.
C.V.O.	1¾in.	1¼in.
L.V.O.	1¼in.	1¼in.
M.V.O.	1¼in.	1¼in.
R.V.M.	1¼in.	1¼in.
G.B.E.	4in.	1½in.
Dames Grand Cross (G.B.E.)	2¼in.	1½in.
K.B.E.	1¾in.	1½in.
D.B.E.	1¾in.	1½in.
C.B.E.	1¾in.	1½in.
O.B.E.	1½in.	1½in.
M.B.E.	1½in.	1½in.
B.E.M.	1¼in.	1¼in.
Companion of Honour	1½in.	1½in.
Distinguished Service Order	1⅛in.	1⅛in.
Crown of India	1½in.	1½in.
Baronet's Badge	1¾in.	Not worn
Order of St. John:		
Bailiffs Grand Cross	4in.	1½in.
Dames Grand Cross	2¼in.	1½in.
Knights of Justice	2in.	1½in.
Dames of Justice	1¼in.	1¼in.
Knights of Grace	2in.	1½in.
Dames of Grace	1¼in.	1¼in.

Chaplain	2in.	1½in.
Commander (Brother)	1½in.	1½in.
Commander (Sister)	1¼in.	1¼in.
Officer (Brother)	1½in.	1½in.
Officer (Sister)	1¼in.	1¼in.
Serving Brother	1½in.	1½in.
Serving Sister	1¼in.	1¼in.

6. Riband bar emblems
(see diagrams page 60)

These are small emblems that are attached to the riband when ribands only are being worn and take the form of a metal rosette or another design relative to the Order, Decoration or Medal being represented.

Silver Rosettes
These are the most common type of emblem which are used for riband bars and are used to denote the following:-

(a) That the wearer has received a second award of their gallantry decoration for subsequent acts of bravery or the case of a long service medal with additional bar to denote a further number of years service.

(b) On World War II campaign stars to denote that the wearer was present at an additional theatre of operation not represented by a riband. In the case of the 1939-45 Star, recipients of the clasp 'Battle of Britain' wear a gilt rosette on the riband (see page 45).

Recipients of the Victoria and George Crosses wear a miniature replica of the Cross on the riband when ribands only are worn. Servicemen entitled to the Africa Star and who served in either the 1st or 8th armies will wear either a numeral 1 or 8 on their riband bars. In the case of the South Atlantic Medal 1982, a rosette is worn on the riband to denote service of one day in the Falkland Islands or their Dependencies or in the South Atlantic between 35° South and 60° South, or in any operational sortie south of Ascension Island. Multiple clasps awarded to the General Service Medals do not carry rosettes therefore a plain riband only is worn.

7. Foreign Rosettes

In the case of Foreign Orders, rosettes can be worn to denote the class of the Order. In addition to the rosette being worn on the riband bar an example of the rosette may be worn in the buttonhole while the wearer is in everyday dress.

To denote the multiple classes of an Order, a coloured flash or knot is often used protruding from each side behind the rosette, the colours of the flashes are as follows:-

All gold	1st class, Grand Cross
Half gold, half silver	2nd class, Knight Commander
All silver	3rd class, Commander
No flash	4th class, Officer
Lapel clip narrow riband	5th class, Member

8. Mention in Despatches

In 1920 King George V approved that an emblem should be worn on the WWI Victory Medal riband to denote a person being mentioned in wartime despatches. The emblem was to take the form of a multiple leaved bronze oak leaf. Only one emblem was to be worn, irrespective of the number of times any individual had been mentioned.

Mention in Despatches 1914-1919

The emblem of bronze oak leaves is worn on the riband of the Victory Medal. The award of this emblem ceased as from 10 August 1920.

Mention in Despatches 1920-1939

The single bronze oak leaf emblem, if granted for service in operations between the two World Wars, is worn on the riband of the appropriate General Service Medal. If a G.S.M. has not been granted, the emblem is worn directly on the coat after any medal ribands. If there are no ribands, it is worn in the position of a single riband.

Mention in Despatches 1939-1945

This single leaved emblem is to be worn on the 1939-45 War Medal, or if this has not been awarded, directly after any medal ribands.

Mention in Despatches subsequent to 1945

The single bronze oak leaf is to be worn on the relevant campaign medal riband. If a medal has not been granted then it is worn directly on the coat after any medal ribands. If there are no ribands, it is worn in the position of a single riband. It should be placed above any clasp or emblem or rosette which is also permitted to be worn on the relevant medal riband.

Mention in despatch emblems are worn on the riband bar and are fixed horizontally across the riband with the stalk furthest from the left shoulder. If the emblem is not worn with a campaign medal, it can be worn after any Order, Decoration or Medal on a piece of cloth covered buckram. The single bronze oak leaf emblem was also granted from the end of the 1939-45 War up to 1952 to denote a Queen's Commendation for Brave Conduct, and Queen's Commendation for Valuable Services in the Air.

9. South Atlantic Medal

When ribands only are being worn the rosette should be placed farthest from the left shoulder and the oak leaf emblem placed horizontally alongside with the leaves pointing to the left shoulder.

10. King/Queen's Commendation for Brave Conduct

Since 1952 a silver laurel leaved emblem has been granted to civilians only, other than those in the merchant navy. During World War II this emblem was worn on the Defence Medal if appropriate, or it was worn after any medals, or, if no medals had been awarded to the recipient, it was worn in the place of a single medal.

11. Queen's Commendation for Valuable Services in the Air

This award was instituted in 1942 in recognition for gallantry not reaching the required standard to be awarded the Air Force Cross. The oval badge, in silver, is worn on the coat immediately below any medals or ribands. In civilian air line uniform, it is worn on the panel of the left breast pocket.

The Most Noble Order of The Garter

Part of the insignia of The Most Noble Order of The Garter is the actual Garter itself of dark blue velvet and gold bearing the motto 'Honi soit qui mal y pense' in gold lettering.

When the Garter is worn by gentlemen it is positioned below the left knee when in knee breeches. However if it is to be worn by a lady it is positioned on the left arm above the elbow.

The Knight Bachelor's Badge

When a Knight is presented with this award it is in the form of a neck badge being suspended from a riband. However, many Knights are also awarded other neck Orders such as Commander of The British Empire or Companion of the Order of The Bath, and as in most forms of dress only one neck badge may be worn at any one time. The Knight therefore, has to make the decision as to which one of his Orders is the most appropriate to wear.

However, a solution has been found to the problem in that, in addition to the Knight having both Orders being represented on a miniature medal bar, the Imperial Society of Knights Bachelor make available a larger version of the Order badge with a pin fitting on the reverse enabling the Order to be worn in the position of a breast star thus allowing the Knight to be able to wear more than one Order at the same time. The breast badge takes precedence immediately after the badge of the Knight Commander of The Most Excellent Order of The British Empire.

The miniature of the badge may be worn provided that the holder is entitled to wear one or more other Orders, Decorations or Medals.

The Royal Victorian Medal

The Royal Victorian Medal was instituted by Queen Victoria and is a personal award to those who perform outstanding services to the Sovereign or other members of the Royal Family.

The medal has three categories—gold, silver and bronze. Any person who receives a medal of more than one category shall wear them on a medal bar side by side. Any subsequent award of the same type shall be recorded by means of a clasp attached either to the riband bar (men), or to the centre of the bow from which the medal is suspended (ladies).

The clasp is inscribed with the year of award and with the Royal Cypher on the reverse.

The medal may also be worn in addition to any class of the Royal Victorian Order that may be subsequently awarded.

The Most Excellent Order of The British Empire

This Order is divided into two divisions, namely, military and civil, and also has five classes in addition to a medal of the Order.

Unlike any of the other Orders, a silver oak leaf emblem was awarded for gallantry between 1957-1974. Classification for the award as having been made for 'gallantry' has no effect upon the seniority or precedence in the various classes of the Order.

A person appointed to the Order between 6 December 1957 and 19 June 1974 'for gallantry', and subsequently promoted in the Order, retains and wears the insignia of the lower class with the emblem, in addition to the insignia of the higher class, whether promoted for gallantry or otherwise. A holder of the British Empire Medal for Gallantry granted between the above dates if subsequently appointed to the Order, continues to wear the emblem on the riband of the medal.

The gallantry emblem for the British Empire Medal for Gallantry is worn on the riband above and 2nd award clasp which may have been awarded, and when ribands are worn alone, the emblem is worn further from the left shoulder than any silver rosette denoting the award of a 2nd clasp.

An additional statute, 7/12/71, was published stating that a person promoted from a lower class in one division to a higher class in the other division, should retain and wear the insignia of the lower class, in addition to that of the higher class.

With the institution of the Queen's Gallantry Medal on 20 June 1974 awards in the Order for Gallantry ceased to be made.

Unofficial Medals

An unofficial medal is the term given to any Order, Decoration or Medal that has been awarded or sold by a service, society or organisation, and not issued by the Crown or government of the country concerned.

Over recent years more and more private societies and organisations have begun to strike their own medals to commemorate specific occasions. Unfortunately however, in some cases recipients of these medals have mounted them alongside their official medals. These medals, whether full size or miniature, are not permitted to be worn mounted with official Orders, Decorations and Medals. The practice of wearing them on Armistice parades and the like, mounted on a separate medal brooch and worn underneath any official medals that the holder is entitled to wear, is not officially recognised.

Abbreviations after names and Post Nominal letters

Abbreviations indicating titles and honours, etc., should be placed in the following order:-

1. The letters 'Bt.' or 'Bart.' for Baronet and 'Esq.' for Esquire come immediately after the name. The latter should never be used if the name is prefixed by a title such as Mr., Colonel, Reverend or Sir, etc.
2. Orders, Decorations and Medals—as per the order shown on page 68.
3. Crown appointments such as PC and ADC.
4. Religious Orders.
5. Academic distinctions and honorary degrees in the order of award.
6. Medical qualifications, excluding degrees.
7. Official appointments.
8. Membership of the Armed Forces.

Post Nominal letters

V.C.
G.C.
K.G.⎫
K.T.⎭ Not used by ladies
K.P.
G.C.B. Also used by ladies
O.M.
G.C.S.I.
G.C.M.G. Also used by ladies
G.C.I.E.
C.I. Ladies only
G.C.V.O. Also used by ladies
G.B.E. Also used by ladies
C.H.
K.C.B.
D.C.B.
K.C.S.I.
K.C.M.G.
D.C.M.G.
K.C.I.E.
K.C.V.O.
D.C.V.O.
K.B.E.
D.B.E.
C.B.
C.S.I.
C.M.G.
C.I.E.
C.V.O.
C.B.E.
D.S.O.
L.V.O.
O.B.E.
Q.S.O.
I.S.O.
M.V.O.
M.B.E.
I.O.M. (military)
O.B.—gallantry
R.R.C.
D.S.C.
M.C.

D.F.C.
A.F.C.
A.R.R.C.
O.B.I.
O.B.—distinguished service
A.M.
D.C.M.
C.G.M.
G.M.
Q.P.M.—gallantry
Q.F.S.M.—gallantry
E.M.
D.C.M.—West Africa Frontier Force
D.C.M.—Kings African Rifles
I.D.S.M.
B.G.M.
D.S.M.
M.M.
D.F.M.
A.F.M.
S.G.M.
I.O.M. (Civil)
C.P.M.—gallantry
Q.G.M.
Q.S.M.
R.V.M.
B.E.M.
C.M. or M du C
Q.P.M.—distinguished service
Q.F.S.M.—distinguished service
C.P.M.S.M.
M.S.M.—only if awarded in Navy
              prior to 20/7/28
E.R.D.
V.D.
T.D.
E.D.
R.D.
V.R.D.
A.E.A.⎫
U.D.R.⎭ Officers only
C.D.

Regulations for the return of the Insignia of Orders on the promotion or death of a member

On promotion to a higher class of an Order, the insignia of the lower class should be returned to the Secretary of The Central Chancery of the Orders of Knighthood at St. James's Palace.

In the event of the death of a member of any of the Orders, the following practices should be observed in accordance with statutory law.

The Most Noble Order of The Garter, and The Most Ancient and Most Noble Order of The Thistle

The badge and Star are delivered up by the Knight's nearest living male relative to the Sovereign of the Order. The collar, with badge appendant, should be returned to the Secretary of The Central Chancery of the Orders of Knighthood.

The Most Honourable Order of The Bath

G.C.B. — The collar with the badge appendant are returnable to The Central Chancery of the Orders of Knighthood. The Order badge and breast star are not returnable.

K.C.B. — The Order badge and star are not returnable.

C.B. — The Order badge is not returnable.

The Order of Merit

The Order badge is not returnable.

The Most Distinguished Order of St. Michael and St. George

G.C.M.G. — since 1948 the collar only has been returnable

K.C.M.G. }
C.M.G. } neither of these classes are returnable

The Victorian Chain

The Royal Victorian Chain should be returned to the Secretary of The Central Chancery of the Orders of Knighthood.

The Royal Victorian Order

G.C.V.O. — the collar is returned to The Central Chancery of the Orders of Knighthood, but Order badge and breast star are not returnable.

K.C.V.O. ⎫
C.V.O. ⎬ none of these classes are returnable
L.V.O. ⎪
M.V.O. ⎭

The Most Excellent Order of The British Empire

G.B.E. — The collar is returned to The Central Chancery of the Orders of Knighthood, but the Order badge and breast star are not returnable.

K.B.E. ⎫
D.B.E. ⎪
C.B.E. ⎬ none of these classes are returnable
O.B.E. ⎪
M.B.E. ⎭

The Order of the Companion of Honour
The Distinguished Service Order
The Imperial Service Order

None of the above three Orders are returnable.

Useful addresses

Army Medal Department
Ministry of Defence
Worcester Road
Droitwich
Worcestershire
WR9 8AU
Tel. 0905 772323

Army Records Office
Bourne Avenue
Hayes
Middlesex   UB3 1PR

Imperial Society of Knights Bachelor
21 Old Building
Lincoln's Inn
London
WC2

Liverpool Shipwreck and Humane Society
Oriel Chambers
14 Water Street
Liverpool
L2

Lloyd's of London
Lime Street
London
EC3

Naval Medal Department
NPP 4B (ACS 334)
HMS Centurion
Grange Road
Gosport
Hampshire
PO13 9XA
Tel. 0705 822351 X 2204

Public Records Office
Ruskin Avenue
Kew
Richmond
Surrey
Tel. 01-876 3444

72

Royal Air Force Medal Office
R.A.F. Innsworth
Gloucestershire

Rescue Records Supervisor
RNLI
West Quay Road
Poole
Dorset
BH15 1HZ

Royal Humane Society
Brettenham House
Lancaster Place
London
WC2E 7EP

Spink & Son Ltd. (Medallists)
5, 6 & 7
King Street
St. James's
London
SW1Y 6QS
Tel. 01-930 7888

The Central Chancery of the Orders of Knighthood
St. James's Palace
London
SW1A 1BG
Tel. 01-834 2837   *0171 930 4832*

VC and GC Association
Room 04
Archway Block South
Old Admiralty Building
Whitehall
London
SW1
Tel. 01-930 3506

SPINK & SON

Founded 1666

OFFER THE FOLLOWING SERVICES:

Outright purchase of individual works of art or whole collections for cash

Sales in our galleries, *on a commission basis,* either of individual pieces or whole collections

Advice and purchase at auction sales on customers' behalf

Specialist restoration of antique furniture, including carving and gilding (telephone 01-370 4170)

Guidance on the skilful restoration of most works of art

Publications
Octagon—House Magazine

Numismatic Circular—
including Medals, Coins and Banknotes

Periodic Book Catalogue—
Available from the Book Department

Departments; apart from the most comprehensive Medal Department in the world—
including:
Oriental Art
Indian and South-East
Asian Art
Islamic Art
English Paintings and Watercolours
Silver and Jewellery
Paperweights and 19th Century Glass
Ancient, Medieval and Modern Coins
Banknotes
Bullion (Modern gold coins)
Auctioneers

A selection of countries for
which Spink have created and
produced Orders, Decorations and Medals:

Abu Dhabi	Guyana	
Aden	Holland	Pahang
Alberta	Indian Princely States	Pakistan
Bahamas	Iraq	Papua New Guinea
Bahrain	Jamaica	Poland
Bermuda	Kedah	Qatar
Bhutan	Kenya	Ras al Khaimah
Botswana	Kuwait	Roumania
Brazil	Lesotho	Sabah
Brunei	Liberia	Sarawak
Burma	Libya	Selangor
Canada	Luxembourg	Sierra Leone
Czechoslovakia	Malawi	Sikkim
Dubai	Malta	Singapore
Ethiopia	Muscat	Solomon Islands
Fiji	Negri Sembilan	Sudan
France	New Zealand	Tanzania
Gambia	Nigeria	Uganda
Ghana	Norway	United Arab Emirates
Greece	Oman	United Kingdom

MEDALS
SURPLUS TO YOUR REQUIREMENTS

Spink & Son Ltd will be honoured to sell at auction
or make an offer for surplus Orders, Decorations and
Medals, both British and Foreign that you might have
for disposal, whether they be individual pieces,
groups or whole collections.

NOTES

NOTES